A souvenir guide

Dudmaston
Shropshire

Bridget Cherry

National Trust

Ancient and Modern

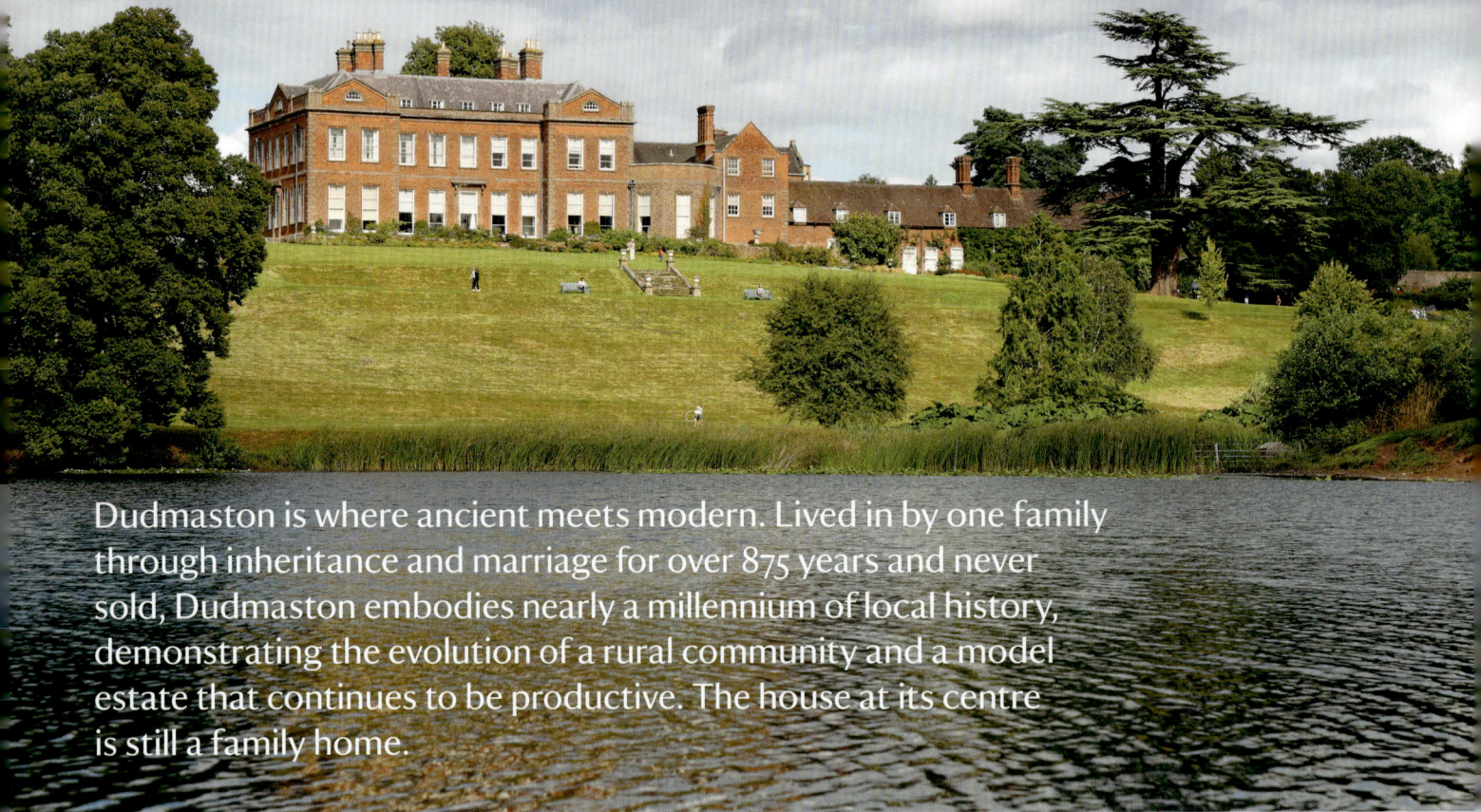

Dudmaston is where ancient meets modern. Lived in by one family through inheritance and marriage for over 875 years and never sold, Dudmaston embodies nearly a millennium of local history, demonstrating the evolution of a rural community and a model estate that continues to be productive. The house at its centre is still a family home.

Over the centuries each generation of the Wolryche and Wolryche-Whitmore family has made its own contribution, all of which can still be enjoyed today: a handsome Baroque mansion of 1700; a picturesque landscape created to exploit the dramatic topography, with its distant views, water features and hidden valley; progressive agricultural improvements during the Age of Enlightenment; Victorian floral showmanship; and perhaps most remarkably of all, the commercial forestry introduced by Geoffrey Wolryche-Whitmore. Forestry rescued Dudmaston from decline in the 20th century and remains a mainstay of current management, balanced by a sensitive appreciation of earlier achievements.

Above The house from across the Big Pool, created from three smaller lakes between 1818 and 1850

Dudmaston Hall is likewise an intriguing combination. The sober panelled rooms of the original house by the architect Francis Smith of Warwick contrast with the Inner Hall and Library remodelled in a lighter Regency style in the early 19th century. Dark oak panels contrast with minimalist whiteness. Family portraits are a reminder of the varied characters and fortunes of the owners. But the furnishings and collections reflect the interests of Sir George and Lady Labouchere, who in 1966 retired to Dudmaston, Lady Labouchere's family home, and took on the task of preparing the house for its new role as a National Trust property. Family heirlooms have been complemented by sympathetic new acquisitions and enhanced by special collections – Lady Labouchere's exquisite examples of botanic art and the outstanding collection of Modern Art made by Sir George when he was British ambassador in Belgium and Spain. This unique combination gives Dudmaston a very special character.

Left Sir George and Lady Labouchere in the grounds

Far left The architect, Francis Smith of Warwick (1672–1738)

Below Autumn leaves by the botanical artist Pandora Sellars (1936–2017), 1975

Dudmaston: the People and the Place

Dudmaston first appears in a deed of c. 1127 when Helgor of Holgate granted a manor called Dodemannestone with half a hide of land to a Norman knight, Harlewyn de Butailles, whose family then adopted the local name of Dudmaston.

The Wolryches arrived on the scene nearly three centuries later, when in 1403 the heiress Margaret de Dudmaston married William Wolryche of Much Wenlock. Their son Andrew was a Member of Parliament for Bridgnorth in 1435, the first of many Wolryche MPs.

The oldest family portrait at Dudmaston is of Francis Wolryche (1563–1614). He was the eighth generation to be descended in a direct line from the marriage of 1403, and was only a small child when he succeeded his father in 1566 as head of the Wolryche family. The portrait showing a serious young man wearing an elegant lace collar was painted in 1591 when he was 28.

Right Sir Francis Wolryche, painted in 1591 at the age of 28

We do not know how Francis was brought up, but in 1588, at the age of 25, he married into the world of high-flying Elizabethan lawyers and politicians, a connection that was to prove important for the next generation. His wife was Margaret Bromley, youngest daughter of Sir George Bromley of Hallon in Worfield, a manor north-east of Bridgnorth. Margaret's uncle was Lord Chancellor, her father was a Member of Parliament, member of the Council of the Marches and Chief Justice of Chester. Francis and Margaret had nine children, of whom two sons and three daughters were alive when Francis died in 1614, aged 50.

The Wolryches' rising status is indicated by the elaborate alabaster tomb in Quatt church, with effigies of Francis and Margaret and figures of their children around the tomb chest. The heraldry demonstrates the importance given to family connections: over a dozen other families are represented in addition to the Wolryche arms (a chevron and three swans on a blue ground). Gentry families built up their estates through marriage, and family links created networks of support in both public and private life. The inscription makes clear that it was the widow who was responsible for the tomb, who '…in a doleful duty doth dedicate this monument to her deare husband…'. In old age Margaret added a simple memorial to her second son George, who died in 1641, with the touching inscription 'mater posuit' (mother placed [it]).

Evidence for the kind of house this large family occupied is sparse. Its character and even its exact site remain a mystery, despite recent archaeological surveys. An early map shows a drive west from the road, still visible as raised ground, leading to the present orchard. Remains of a Tudor garden pavement found in the present rose border suggest the old house was nearby. There is evidence for a steep stone-tiled roof and small diamond-paned windows, and a massive ancient beam has been reused between a corridor and the later kitchen. By the time of the Hearth Tax of 1672 the house had 24 hearths, one of the highest figures in the county, though this could have been due in part to enlargements in the 17th century.

Above left The largely Georgian St Andrew's Church at Quatt contains many Wolryche funerary monuments

Above The figures of Francis and Margaret Wolryche on their tomb in St Andrew's. Their nine children are shown around the sides

Below The Wolryche arms of a chevron between three swans

Sir Thomas Wolryche (1598–1668) and the Civil War

Francis Wolryche's oldest son Thomas was 16 when his father died. Thomas was studying at Cambridge, where, according to the long Latin inscription on his tomb, he was an eager student of geometry, history and heraldry. He was taken under the wing of his uncle, the Exchequer lawyer Edward Bromley, who was a trustee of the estate under Francis Wolryche's will.

He secured Thomas's admission to the Inner Temple in preparation for a legal and political career, and, as Recorder for Much Wenlock, Bromley also supported his election to Parliament. Thomas was MP for Much Wenlock in 1621, 1624 and 1625, but his opportunities for making a name for himself in this field were limited. As opposition increased to Charles I's autocratic rule without Parliament, the country gentry began to take sides. After Bromley's death in 1626, Thomas allied himself with the leader of the Royalists at Shrewsbury, his brother-in-law Francis Ottley, whose sister Ursula he had married in 1625. In 1641 when the king sought to raise funds for possible military action, Thomas Wolryche was among those who offered support, and acquired a baronetcy as a reward. He accepted a commission to collect taxes for the king, received a Commission of Array to raise soldiers, and probably due to Ottley was made governor of Bridgnorth Castle.

He was replaced as governor around 1644 and was not present at the dramatic siege of Bridgnorth, when the town was eventually captured by the Parliamentarians in 1646.

He then accepted the new regime and paid the required taxes, but Royalists were threatened with the confiscation of their lands unless they 'compounded' – made a payment based on a valuation of their property. Sir Thomas was given a lenient fine, paying £730, one-tenth of the value of his estate at Dudmaston together with land in a dozen other places, some of it quite recently acquired. The decision was no doubt helped by the evidence he submitted, that he had laid down arms before 1 March 1644, and as the Bailiffs of Bridgnorth put it:

'for ought we know never after did beare arms but lived peacably at his said habitation at Dudmaston'.

Below Only the keep of Bridgnorth Castle survived the Civil War, despite leaning at 15 degrees

KEEP OF BRIDGENORTH CASTLE,
Built by Robert of Belesme.

Right Ursula Ottley, daughter of Thomas Ottley of Pitchford Hall, married Sir Thomas in 1625

But life for him and his young family – over 20 years 12 children had been born to him and Ursula – was not straightforward. According to the inscription on his tomb, Sir Thomas suffered imprisonment; he was able to pay the fine only gradually, and there were reports of the County Committee ignoring instructions from London and seizing his rents and cattle.

He survived to see the monarchy restored and his estates secure, and died aged 70 in 1668. His wife erected a grand marble chest tomb at Quatt; the inscription recording his life expressed his pride not only in his ennoblement and public service but in sending six sons to Cambridge University where he himself had studied.

The later 17th century

Francis, the eldest son of Sir Thomas, studied at Cambridge and inherited in 1668 at the age of 41, but proved incapable, and was declared a lunatic.

By an Act of Parliament in 1673 he retained the title until his death in 1689, but the estate was settled on his younger brother John, a lawyer who was a member of Gray's Inn and, like his father, was elected MP for Much Wenlock. He married Mary Griffith, the daughter of the royal chaplain Matthew Griffith.

Mary was a talented musician, 'outstanding in her singing and the playing of the lyre', but sadly died in childbirth in 1678; a monument to her at Quatt, ascribed to the London sculptor Jasper Latham, shows her reclining in a fashionable *décolleté* dress, holding a lute. John's up-to-date taste may also be reflected in the unusually ornate 'New House' (now Dower House) opposite Quatt church. Was it intended as a residence while the main house was rebuilt? The extension of the brewhouse, with its bell dated 1680, suggests building work was in hand. But before the house at Quatt was completed, John died of smallpox in 1685, at the age of 48.

Above Sir Francis Wolryche, 2nd Bt, c. 1650

Below The massive monument in St Andrew's to Mary Griffith (d.1678), holding a lute

The new Dudmaston House

Sir Thomas Wolryche, 3rd Bt (1672–1701) was only 13 when he inherited, and any plans for rebuilding were put on hold. It was his marriage to Elizabeth Weld in 1689 which prompted action, as indicated by a letter of 10 April 1695 from his father-in-law, George Weld of Willey (MP for Much Wenlock) to Andrew Archer of Umberslade, Warwickshire:

Sir, Having had ye honr to sitt with you in the House of Commons makes me soe bold to beg of you that if you have a modell of your House you will lend it to Sir Tho. Wolryche my Son in Lawe for some time, and I will carefully Returne it to you againe, if you have not such a modell, that then you will lett this bearer take a platt of ye same.

The word 'platt' indicates a design on paper. The letter provides evidence for the involvement of the Midlands master builder and architect Francis Smith. The new Dudmaston House resembles Umberslade and other early houses by Smith. The plainly detailed symmetrical brick exterior is given dignity by a ground floor raised over a basement (on the garden side this is now obscured by later terracing). Before the top floor was altered, the house was of two main storeys, with attics within a hipped roof. The compact design, two rooms deep in the centre, with projecting three-room wings, followed current fashion, with the hall in the centre block leading to a room facing the garden. The Entrance Hall, with its full-height panelling, and the Oak Room in the south-west corner of the house still convey the sober splendour of the early 18th-century building. Spacious basements included capacious vaulted wine cellars; kitchen and service rooms were in lower buildings to the south, perhaps making use of older structures and materials.

Top The Entrance Hall with 17th-century refectory table

Above The Oak Room has its original 18th-century panelling, fitted at the same time as the Entrance Hall

The last Wolryches

Before Sir Thomas's fine new house was completed, tragedy struck; he died from tuberculosis at the age of only 29 and the title passed to his ten-year-old son. John, 4th Bt grew up to be an irresponsible spendthrift, passionately involved in horse-racing, hunting and cockfighting.

In 1723, after celebrating a winning day at the Chelmarsh races, he was drowned while trying to ford the River Severn on his way home. From his time dates the portrait known as the 'Wolryche Fool' attributed to the local artist George Alsop, displaying the grand ale glass thought to be

associated with the Wolryche hunt, and two other portraits of servants. Were they painted to commemorate the riotous life at Dudmaston?

The estate, left with heavy debts and no male heir, was eventually settled in 1741 on John's sister Mary after payment of debts of £14,000. Mary managed the estate with the help of her mother and her uncle, Colonel Thomas Weld, a younger son of George Weld of Willey. He had been a soldier fighting with the Duke of Marlborough, and briefly, MP for Much Wenlock, before retiring to live with his sister. His epitaph at Quatt notes that 'his polite and

Above An oil painting attributed to George Alsop (fl.1722–30) known as *'Portrait of the Wolryche Fool as an Old Man'*, depicting the Wolryche Hunt servant with the Dudmaston Ale Glass

Left *The Dudmaston Gamekeeper*, possibly George Griffith, and possibly also by George Alsop

cheerful conversation procured him the love and esteem of a very extensive acquaintance' and 'his charity and benevolence the good wishes and sincere prayers of the poor'. Good works included improvements to Quatt church in 1763. The house was maintained, though 'unfinished' rooms mentioned in an inventory of 1774 suggest only partial occupation by that time. But for nearly 40 years traditional if frugal hospitality was offered, as described in an account from the 1750s:

Dinner was ready every day at one o'clock for twenty persons, and when the bell rang any neighbouring farmers out working in their fields were welcome to come and any friends of the family who chose to partake of the plain hospitable dinner provided. Those who came in time sat down with Colonel Weld and his sister lady Woolridge [sic], those who were late partook with the servants and after all had dined the remains were given to the poor… When prayers were over, they went to dinner. The colonel brought always a bottle of wine from which you were expected to drink one glass, if you took more it was more than was expected, or desired, but there was plenty of Ale. When Lady Woolridge was able to come into Company she went after dinner to a closet in the room and brought a bottle of port with her from which you were likewise asked to have one glass.

Lady Wolryche died in 1765 aged 92 'having lived a widow for 64 years', as is stated on the elegant memorial erected by her daughter Mary. Mary died in 1771, leaving the estate in trust, legacies to her cousins, and gold, silver, carriages and horses to Mary Gatacre (probably the daughter of Colonel Weld), who had lived at Dudmaston from 1728. The estate passed to the nonagenarian Colonel, who died in 1774, bequeathing Dudmaston to a distant cousin, George Whitmore.

Above *Sir John Wolryche's Hunt,* British (English) School, c. 1712/20. Hounds, hunstmen and servants are shown in a stylised landscape representing the River Severn and Bridgnorth high town in the background. The figure in white is probably the extravagant Sir John, who loved hunting, horse-racing and cock-fighting and spent large sums on these sports. The presence of the river is significant, as Sir John drowned trying to cross it on his way home after celebrating too well a winning day at Chelmarsh races, leaving Dudmaston with crippling debts

The Whitmores

The direct line of the Wolryche family ended with the death of Mary. The new owner from 1775, a nephew of George Whitmore, was William Whitmore (1745–1815), the 30-year-old son of a Southampton wine merchant. He found little in the house; furniture and silver had been given away.

Below William Emes's plan for Dudmaston, 1777

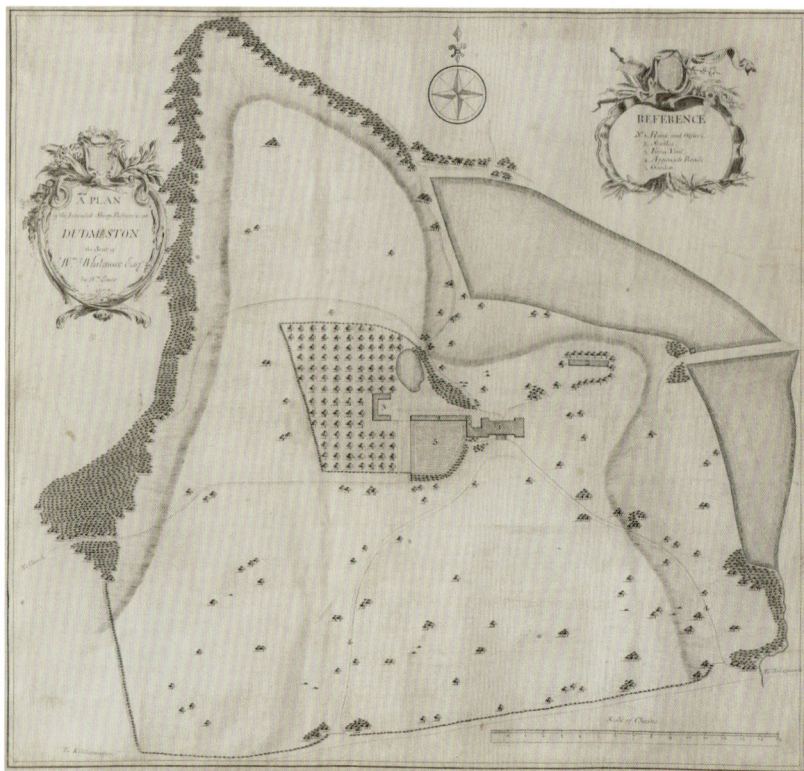

William's experiences were later recounted by his daughter Frances: 'My father found Dudmaston a large and in some parts unfinished house quite empty. I have heard him say he could find nothing when he took possession – but an old pair of yellow breeches in a large antique oaken chest…'

William Whitmore was fortunate in inheriting other estates in Shropshire, at Leebotwood and Woolstaston. Though he assumed Wolryche as his middle name, placing the initials WWW on the stables for example, he never adopted it legally. He married Frances Lister whom he had met at the Shrewsbury races, according to their daughter. He could afford to furnish and repair the house and he brought new vigour to the management of the estate, adopting the latest progressive agricultural practices. Up-to-date techniques such as improved drainage and manuring were introduced, together with new threshing machines, and in the 1780s he added to the agricultural land by enclosing part of Morfe Heath. He added new stables and an extension to the brewhouse, and made a start on the rebuilding of the Dudmaston farms.

A surviving steward's book records that in 1776, out of a total expenditure of £2,972 he spent £420 on building the house, barn and stables at Lodge Farm, £421 on farming and £81 on improvements. But William combined practicality with aesthetics. Lodge Farm, visible when one looked across a pool from the mansion, was given a castellated outline and Tudor window surrounds, providing an interesting

viewpoint in the spirit of the newly fashionable Picturesque movement. The following year William commissioned 'a plan of the intended sheep pasture about Dudmaston' from the landscape architect William Emes, who had built up a successful practice in the Midlands, applying the principles of 'Capability' Brown to current farming methods. The plan showed house and outbuildings in an enclosure surrounded by pasture crossed by winding paths; although it was not carried out, the concept of the house looking out over water and open landscape influenced later developments. Contrasting with this was the creation of the romantically picturesque Dingle, which was undertaken by the gardener Walter Wood, together with Frances Whitmore (see p.32).

William and his wife Frances had six daughters and then a son, William, who was given the ancient family name of Wolryche as a second baptismal name. He was followed by three more daughters before Frances died in 1792, aged only 42. William married again and had children with his second wife, Marie Louisa Thomas.

(see p.32).

Above left Door decorated by Mary Dorothea Whitmore

Above *Mary Dorothea Whitmore*, Mrs Francis Laing (1781–1872), English School, c. 1820–30. A half-length portrait of the wife of the Reverend Francis Laing and sister of William Wolryche-Whitmore

William Wolryche-Whitmore

William Wolryche-Whitmore (1787–1858) inherited Dudmaston on his father's death in 1815. In 1805 he had married Lucy Bridgeman, daughter of the Earl of Bradford, who brought a welcome dowry. The young couple were among those who seized the opportunity to travel abroad as the Napoleonic Wars were ending, and their continental tour in 1814 even included a visit to Napoleon in exile.

From 1820 to 1832 Wolryche-Whitmore followed the Dudmaston tradition as MP for Bridgnorth, but his progressive views on Catholic emancipation and anti-slavery petitions, and above all his campaign for free trade, distanced him from the Shropshire gentry. His monument records that 'repeated defeats by large majorities, the faint support of friends, the reproaches of his own class failed to daunt him in the faithful discharge of this public duty'. From 1832 to 1835 he represented the new constituency of Wolverhampton in the hope that urban voters would be more sympathetic. In Parliament he was a forthright if rather pompous speaker, criticised for 'his habit of lifting his arms above his head à la Irving which often gives a notion of solemnity not well suited to everyday matters of business', but William Wilberforce, meeting him on his home ground, was surprised to find 'a kindness and generosity unassuming and great, and a modesty and humility truly delightful to witness'.

The young couple clearly found Dudmaston gloomy and old-fashioned, and in the 1820s alterations were put in hand by the local builder, John Smalman of Quatford. The attic floor was rebuilt and embellished with pedimental gables in Neo-classical taste. A light and airy main staircase was created in what was then the south wing, with cantilevered stone steps and wrought-iron balustrade. A Library with delicate built-in bookcases, inspired by those in Lucy's much grander former home, Weston Park in Staffordshire, was created from two rooms overlooking the garden. The lengthened Library windows opened on to a low terrace with a fine view over the enlarged lake and parkland beyond. Entertainment facilities were improved by a new dining-room overlooking the garden, added in 1833, with remodelled service buildings.

An innovative central heating system was installed, designed by Wolryche-Whitmore's brother-in-law, the computer pioneer Charles Babbage.

Much was done to bring the garden near the house in line with current taste by creating a rock garden around an existing stone outcrop, an 'American garden' with exotic plants from the New World, and bedding plants in elaborate designs (see p.29). In contrast, contemporary views show parkland around the house much on the lines of Emes's earlier proposal. The estate improvements instigated by William Whitmore were continued – new farm buildings, the enclosure of Morfe Heath (begun in the 1780s), drainage work, and the use of bone-based manure and other fertilisers to make the land more productive. But it all came at a cost: mortgages of £60,000 when Wolryche-Whitmore died in 1858.

Above left Silhouette drawing of William Wolryche-Whitmore, 1815

Above right Lady Lucy Bridgeman, daughter of Orlando 1st Earl of Bradford of the second creation (1815) and his wife the Hon. Lucy Byng

Opposite above The Inner Hall created by John Smalman in the 1820s. The stone stairs are skilfully cantilevered

Opposite below The Library, created from two rooms by John Smalman in the 1820s

The later 19th and 20th centuries

Above The north and garden fronts of the house before the terraces were built by William Wolryche-Whitmore between 1818 and 1850

Right The Victorian clock tower was built to house an older bell of 1680. It forms part of the extensive group of older service buildings south east of the house

William Wolryche-Whitmore died in 1858 leaving Dudmaston to his brother-in-law, the Rev. Francis Laing, vicar of Quatt, who was married to Mary Dorothea, William's sister. The house was let to an Australian sheep farmer, and it was only in 1864 that it was again occupied by the family.

By then the Rev. Francis Henry Laing had succeeded his father as owner, and he marked his acceptance of the role by adopting the Wolryche-Whitmore name. He and his wife Isabella both lived into the early 20th century, dying at the ages of 88 and 91. Despite the hard times of the agricultural depression from 1873, almost all the debts had been paid off by 1900. The gardens were simplified but kept in good order, and the woodlands were managed for sport.

Money was found for another wave of picturesque improvements: entrance lodges, a clock-tower by the stables, and at Quatt, an attractive set of cottages along the main road.

Francis Alexander Wolryche-Whitmore, Francis and Isabella's son, inherited the estate in 1908 but he and his wife Alice (1852–1931) already had Larden Hall near Much Wenlock and a London house and were only at Dudmaston from 1912 to 1921. Alice Darby's distinguished forebears had significance for Dudmaston; she brought to the house fine china and works of art, including early botanical paintings. Many were inherited from her paternal family, the Darbys of Coalbrookdale, the Quaker ironmasters who pioneered Shropshire industry. Other treasures came from her mother's family, the Christys.

Alice's granddaughter Rachel (born 1908), the later owner of Dudmaston, had happy memories of her childhood visits, recalling the family portraits, tea in the housekeeper's room, and the character given to the house by its ornaments and pictures.

She also remembered the enthusiasm for gardening shared by her grandmother and aunt Muriel (see p.19), her uncle Geoffrey's second wife. Geoffrey's two sisters were Olive, Rachel's mother, who had married Eustace Scott Hamilton-Russell, younger son of Viscount Boyne, who had grown up at nearby Burwarton, and Frances Evelyn (1872–1948), who married George Blacklock, and under the name Evelyn Blacklock became a distinguished artist. She was often at Dudmaston, and her paintings of country scenes, horses and family portraits convey a sense of comfortable rural tranquillity, but one which became increasingly fragile after the start of the First World War.

Above left The Rev. Francis Henry Laing who took the Wolryche-Whitmore name in 1864 and paid off the estate's debts

Above Francis Alexander Wolryche-Whitmore inherited Dudmaston from his father in 1908 and immediately appointed his son Geoffrey as agent

Captain Geoffrey Wolryche-Whitmore

Geoffrey Charlton Wolryche-Whitmore (1881–1969) became the agent of the estate in 1908 at the age of 27, having trained on the progressive estates of Apethorpe in Northamptonshire and Buscot Park in Oxfordshire.

Looking back on that period, he wrote in 1962 to his niece Rachel about 'the nightmare' that Dudmaston had presented to his grandfather, his father and himself, with farms let and changing hands repeatedly, the problem of rabbits, low corn prices, no machinery and no market for timber except large hardwoods.

Full of enthusiasm for his new role, he travelled to Germany to study modern methods of forestry, with the aim of making the Dudmaston estate an economic success. In 1910 he planted 80 hectares (200 acres) of woodland on sandy soil not suitable for farming, and established a sawmill at Holt, with saws powered by a paraffin Crossley engine. Previously all timber had been cut by hand at the felling site by itinerant foresters, but Dudmaston now began to employ a permanent staff of woodmen and carpenters.

Before the effects could be appreciated, war intervened. Geoffrey had been a lieutenant in the Shropshire Yeomanry, and in 1914 he reported for service two days after war was declared. He was 'glad to go and try and do one's share', and chose to join the 1st Battalion, which would be trained ready to go to the front, although as a member of a territorial unit he could have chosen to serve in England.

After twelve months' training he was posted to Egypt, but never saw any action. He wrote home that the stationmaster at Hampton Loade could have done his job and that 'few first line regiments have been so badly used as ours'. He felt he spent the war in 'the art of doing nothing'. Because of his deafness, in early 1917 he reluctantly left his regiment for a job teaching officers topography. He came home in 1919, with an unjustified feeling of worthlessness and that he never 'did his bit'.

A second marriage

He married his second wife, Muriel Murray, in 1919 (his first wife, Susan Lethbridge, had died soon after their marriage in 1907); Muriel was the widow of his dear friend Algie who was killed in action. Geoffrey threw himself back into the management of Dudmaston with great success; he was a conscientious landlord and there were improvements which benefited the tenants, such as the three hydraulic rams installed to provide water for farms and for the houses in Quatt village, all previously reliant on wells.

Opposite Captain Geoffrey Wolryche-Whitmore in uniform during the First World War

Left Estate woodmen

Above Geoffrey Wolryche-Whitmore in the Corsican pine plantation. Besides his progressive methods, he invented new tools such as the Whitmore pruning chisel and the ladder saddle

Lady Labouchere
and Sir George

Geoffrey Wolryche-Whitmore had no
children. It was agreed in 1952 that
Dudmaston would be inherited by his niece
Rachel, with the understanding that the
estate would ultimately pass to the National
Trust. But for Rachel, Dudmaston was
a distant dream for many years.

In 1943 she had married a diplomat, George Labouchere, whom she had met in 1940 while working at the Admiralty. She travelled the world as a busy diplomat's wife – first in war-time Sweden, then in Nanking, Buenos Aires, Vienna and Budapest. Her husband, knighted in 1955, was British Ambassador in Brussels from 1956 to 1959, and British Ambassador in Madrid from 1960 to 1966, coping with strained relations between Britain and General Franco. He was described as 'the perfect diplomat, witty, courteous and impeccably groomed', who rarely expressed his personal opinions to the press.

Meanwhile Lady Labouchere developed her interest in painting, especially botanical art, attending classes when possible. Her letters to her parents reveal how she missed the English spring, was reading about her Wolryche and Darby forebears, and was concerned that archives and memories should be preserved.

Both the Laboucheres made efforts to spread interest in British culture; in Sweden they lectured on English country houses and English embroidery. But while Rachel looked back to past traditions, in Brussels Sir George began to develop an interest in collecting Modern Art. His first purchases – small pieces by Henry Moore and Barbara Hepworth, and drawings by other British sculptors – endorsed the British Council's efforts to promote contemporary British sculpture abroad as an expression of humanist values. Grappling with abstract art extended his interest to French and American works. In Spain, more daringly, he developed close links with contemporary Spanish artists, among them the Catalan Antoni Tàpies, whose abstract works in mixed media were esteemed abroad but unacceptable to the Spanish regime. He wrote later that he enjoyed collecting artworks not only because they appealed personally but because they were a way of understanding the countries where he worked. As he developed the idea of making a collection of historical interest, he acquired early works by Sonia Delaunay and Wassily Kandinsky to show that abstract art was a development that had begun in the early 20th century.

In 1966, on Sir George's retirement, the Laboucheres made Dudmaston their home, but with the intention of displaying the house to the public. Parts of the house were redecorated by the interior designer Nina Campbell, though Lady Labouchere chose the paint schemes, especially the white in the Library as a backdrop for pictures. Textiles and wallpaper were supplied by Colefax and Fowler. The family pictures were supplemented by Lady Labouchere's own collection of botanical art (including some of her own drawings) and by Sir George's Modern Art. The art collection was extended by larger works for the grounds by the local sculptor Anthony Twentyman, and by decorative steel gates commissioned from Antony Robinson to celebrate the Laboucheres' Ruby Wedding in 1983.

Opposite left Rachel, Lady Labouchere by the society photographer Dorothy Wilding (1893–1976), 1943

Opposite right The Laboucheres dressed for a Court Ball, spring 1958

Right The Eternity Gates were made of mild steel with applied gold leaf by Antony Robinson and give access to the stable courtyard from the garden

The Art Collection

The paintings and sculpture at Dudmaston are a rare instance
of the donor family consciously building up collections in the subjects
they loved for the benefit of the house and the National Trust.

Modern Art

Sir George Labouchere's collection of 20th-century art was motivated above all by a feeling for beauty. Although he anticipated that some visitors to Dudmaston might be 'shocked' by works that seem to contrast so starkly with the more traditional pictures and sculpture in the house, he hoped that by opening their minds to 'a new way of perceiving beauty' they would share in the 'joy and excitement' that he himself felt in their presence.

Sir George tended to refer to avant-garde art as a source of effervescent delight, comparing the effect of 'going to an exhibition of abstract art' to that of 'a number of very good cocktails'. In keeping with this taste for glamorous modernity, his favourite picture was a jazzy landscape by Jean Dubuffet with the title *Chic Temps,* meaning 'stylish times'. Equally reminiscent of the Laboucheres' heyday in the world of international diplomacy is the dynamic oil painting by Philipp J. Weichberger which evoked for Sir George 'the space and movement of an airport'.

Not wishing anyone to be put off by the non-figurative character of much of his collection, he suggested that we enjoy each work of art with the same attention that we bring to a piece of instrumental music. Barbara Hepworth's *Two Forms,* for example, casts its spell by setting two pieces of highly polished bronze off against each other in a relationship of reflections and curves, shifting and sliding with the movement of the viewer. By contrast, Wassily Kandinsky's *Composition* is all sharply etched lines and spiky angles, creating the impression of speed and electrical energy. Max Ernst's *Coquillage,* meaning 'shell', is a burst of intense colour, bringing to mind the radial striations of a crustacean's shell by the circular application of white over scarlet oil paint. Approached as a unique play of form, texture and colour, every piece in this collection occasions just the kind of 'joy and excitement' in which Sir George hoped we would take part.

Opposite above *Chic Temps* by Jean Dubuffet (1901–85), 1955. This was Sir George's favourite picture in his collection

Opposite below Sir George at his desk surrounded by his collection, including on the right *Composition* by Antoni Clavé (1913–2005), 1960

Below *Coquillage* by Max Ernst (1891–1976), 1961

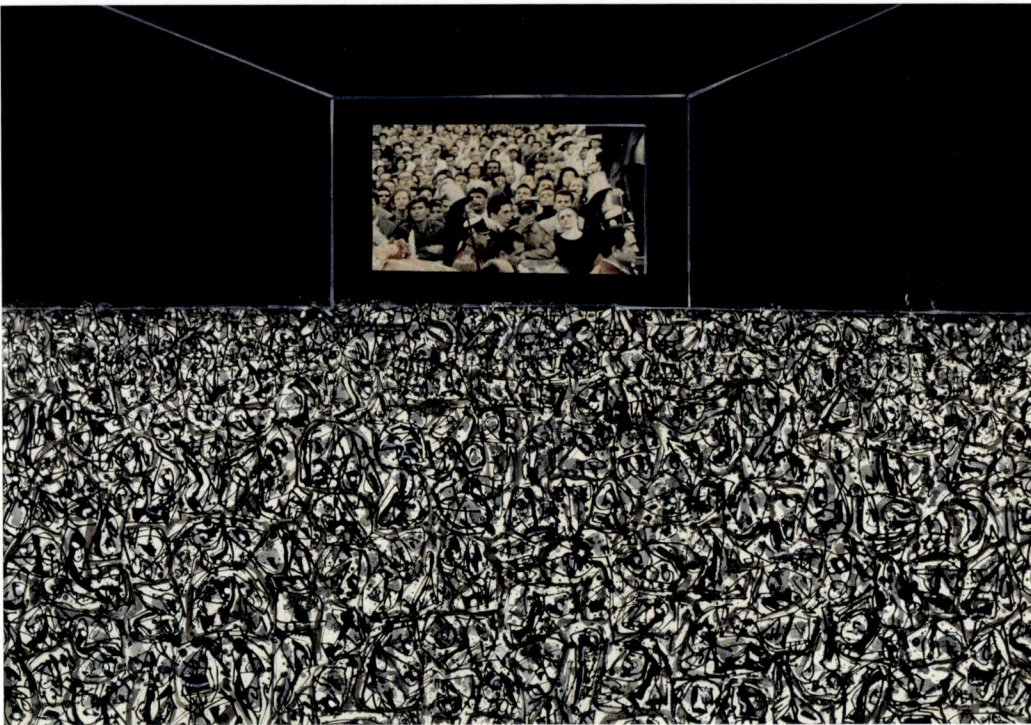

Spanish art

Spanish works of art have an important place in Sir George Labouchere's collection of modern pictures and sculptures, being particularly linked to his diplomatic career. These pieces were collected in the first half of the 1960s when, as British Ambassador in Madrid, he was tasked with maintaining good relations between Great Britain and the authoritarian dictatorship of General Franco.

Sir George was a highly adept diplomat; indeed Franco dubbed him a 'son of Spain', yet his interest as a collector courted controversy – he bought works by young artists who were opposed to the nation's oppressive regime and its parochial and backward art world. Dudmaston has works by each of the manifesto signatories of the short-lived *El Paso* movement (1957–60), meaning 'breakthrough' or 'advance'. Though these works of art are imbued with the grim frustrations of life under dictatorship, look closely and intimations of hope for the future soon become apparent.

Like almost all the Spanish works at Dudmaston, Antonio Saura's *El Cine,* meaning 'the cinema', indicates its serious intentions by the predominant use of black and greys. Saura has created the impression of a film projected onto a cinema screen by pasting a colour photograph onto the inky top half of the picture. The photograph depicts an orderly crowd of people observing the funeral procession of a Catholic cleric escorted by cavalrymen, each representing the most repressive elements of Franco's Spain – the church and military. The cinema audience below is represented by a chaotic pattern of dark lines and masses. Compressed into a rectangle and weighed down by the darkness of the cinema, this other crowd – an image of the real Spanish people – is open to interpretation: as a faceless and cowering mass, or else a restless and interconnected swirl of potential energy, ready to burst free of its bonds.

The suggestion of burgeoning dissent is also present in *Pintura sobre pepel e periodico,* meaning 'painting with newspaper', by the Catalan artist Antoni Tàpies, whose fierce, graffiti-like lines of dark paint evoke the anti-Franco political slogans scrawled around 1960s Spanish cities and roadsides.

Lucio Muñoz painted *Spanish Town* onto a gouged and chiselled-out piece of burnt wood. Though he has literally based his picture on the ruination of Spain's fabric, Muñoz, like his fellow radical artists, nonetheless suggests that hope might be salvaged from destruction through the creation of an original and expressive work of art.

In 1965, while still Ambassador, Sir George allowed his Modern Art collection to be shown at the Museo Nacional Arte Contemporáneo in Madrid. It must surely have been this quality of vigorous optimism that led one reviewer to declare that the exhibition was, above all, 'active and belligerent, open to the future'.

Opposite *El Cine* by Antonio Saura (1930–98), 1963. A vision of Spain under dictatorship

Right *Pintura sobre pepel e periodico* by Antoni Tàpies (1923–2012), 1964, evoking anti-Franco graffiti

Floral art

Lady Labouchere's ancestor, Francis Darby, collected 17th- and 18th-century Dutch flower pieces which came to hang in the Library and Dining Room at Dudmaston.

During a life of travel, Lady Labouchere said that it was 'the flowers by which a special place was often remembered', so it was natural that she should continue to add to the collection.

Dutch flower paintings

Dudmaston houses an exceptional collection of Dutch flower paintings. These were inherited by Lady Labouchere from her Darby relatives, the pioneering industrialist family of nearby Ironbridge, who married into the Wolryche-Whitmores in the 19th century. The fashion for immaculately painted still lifes of flowers developed in the Low Countries in the early 17th century. By the 18th century, when the

pictures at Dudmaston were painted, these floral arrangements had reached the height of exuberance. These brilliantly observed works of art may look very realistic, but they are in fact highly artificial, bringing together varieties that would never have been in bloom at the same time. One of the pieces by Jan van Os includes a bouquet of spring and summer flowers alongside autumnal fruits and game.

Botanical art

Like Sir George, Lady Labouchere was a discerning art collector although her interest was in the tradition of botanical art. As well as acquiring works by the acknowledged masters of the 18th and 19th centuries, she paid close attention to botanical art's 20th-century revival. The collection includes pictures by her friend Mary Grierson, official botanical artist at Kew, and by John Nash, whose courses in flower painting she herself attended at Flatford Mill in Suffolk. For Lady Labouchere, the great value of these sophisticated pictures was the way they led to a more acute feeling for the simple beauties of nature itself:

'In looking carefully at botanical drawing the variety and interesting structure of plants becomes more familiar and so, when seeing all those which daily surround us, it is possible to become more fully aware of unsuspected beauty in the humblest weed. The daisy opening and closing with the changing light and the golden radiance of the dandelion head in sunlight can add a moment of intense pleasure in an ordinary day.'

Opposite above *Still life with Roses, Larkspur and Fruit* by Jan van Os (1744–1808), late 18th century. The painting depicts roses, larkspur and other flowers in a sculpted vase, with fruit including grapes, a pineapple and melon arranged on a stone plinth

Opposite below *Cistus ladanifer* by Mary Grierson (1912–2012), 1974. This flower study incorporates a view of Dudmaston

Right *Still life of Fruit and Flowers* by Jan van Huysum (1682–1749), 1742. This oil painting on copper depicts grapes, pomegranates, red currants and carnations

The Gardens and Estate

Dudmaston's gardens evolved gradually, keeping pace with changing fashion and owing much to the women in the family. Nothing is known of the earliest garden apart from remains of a Tudor path found in the present rose border. Small, formally laid-out plots would have been the fashion up to the early 18th century.

The first significant change came when William Whitmore and his wife Frances reflected the enthusiasm for the new 'Picturesque' fashion that embraced views of the wider landscape. The plan commissioned from William Emes in 1777 showed 'the intended sheep pasture about Dudmaston' with house, orchards and kitchen gardens set in sloping pastures sweeping up to the mansion from the chain of pools that existed to the south. This was not executed at the time, but parkland with mixed clumps of trees was laid out around two new drives from the main road. Between the house and the pools, a stone basin named the 'Ladies' Bath' and a natural outcrop of rock provided points of interest; distant views were countered by the contrast of romantic walks through the Dingle (see p.32).

From the 1820s to the 1850s William Wolryche-Whitmore and his wife Lucy developed the gardens around the house. The steep slope was terraced to provide opportunities for spectacular floral displays, with colourful parterres, island planting beds and specimen conifers. The elaborate carpet bedding designs were celebrated in the *Illustrated London News* in 1851, and the borders 'with nearly a mile of ribbon planting' won a *Gardeners' Chronicle* prize in 1856. The large sandstone outcrop was transformed into a rock garden, and gravelled walks provided links to the new American border planted with fashionable trees and shrubs from the New World. A ha-ha protected this part of the gardens from sheep and cattle. By the mid-19th century three of the small ponds had been united to create the impressive sheet of water known as 'Big Pool'.

Opposite Path beside Big Pool

Above Big Pool

Left The South Lodge in the 1860s. The cruciform-plan lodge dates from the early 19th century and has spirally moulded brick chimneystacks

Simplifying the layout

Left The elaborately planted rockery below the west front of the mansion

Below The west front lawn with island beds and conifers in 1858

In the later 19th century a more economical regime led to a lower-maintenance style: intricate flowerbeds disappeared, although geometric rose beds on the upper terrace remained, together with the lawns set with conifers and yews.

In the early 20th century, Rachel Labouchere remembered her grandmother Alice and her aunt Muriel as keen gardeners who had created the water garden by the Big Pool, now known as the Bog Garden. They had wide interests. They also planted the massive gunneras and bamboos. Alice visited Norway every summer to collect alpines, including the cuckoo flower growing by the brook (*Cardamine raphanifolia*), while Muriel was keen on rock roses and cistus.

The structure of the garden was maintained and new ornamental tree species were introduced. The paved terraces enclosed by low walls next to the house were created in 1920 and the borders filled with madonna lilies.

From the 1960s, Lady Labouchere respected Dudmaston's gardening past, which over time embraced aspects of Picturesque, Regency and Victorian designs, but also made her own modern additions and alterations to the garden, not least by installing some of Sir George Labouchere's abstract sculpture in strategic locations within the garden. She and the garden designer James Russell restyled the herbaceous borders and replanted the house borders with plants of varied origin, while the introduction of modern sculptures provided new points of interest. Dudmaston is therefore a garden which has seen changing fashions and where the old survives alongside the quite unexpected new. The National Trust's recent policy has been to understand and emphasise the interest of the different phases of the garden, for example by repairing the rockery and recovering lost vistas by careful tree thinning.

The Dingle

The Dingle is a steep, wooded valley to the south of the mansion and is perhaps Dudmaston's most striking and important garden feature with waterfalls, rustic bridges and meandering paths.

Frances, daughter of William and Frances Whitmore, described how this became a celebrated part of the garden in the later 18th century, at a time when there was much competition between the country gentry in keeping up with the latest gardening fashions:

The Dingle was a pet of our dear mother's. She laid out the walks therein, placed seats and formed cascades in conjunction with Walter Wood, whom we called Planter, and who was for many years gardener at Dudmaston and died there. This man had imbibed his taste at Shenstone's Leasowes, and the Badger and Dudmaston Dingle were long picturesque rivals. My mother and Aunt Dora were good botanists…

The Leasowes

The poet William Shenstone created one of the most famous 18th-century gardens on his estate at Halesowen (then a part of Shropshire), and was an important influence on Dudmaston. The Leasowes even attracted visits by two future US presidents, Thomas Jefferson and John Adams. It was an admired example of a *ferme ornée:* farmed land where simple rustic walks were given interest by tumbling cascades in a little valley, with carefully placed seats for admiring the views, and inscriptions and poems to encourage contemplation. Shenstone died in 1763. A copy of his posthumously published book outlining his design principles, *Unconnected Thoughts on Gardening,* was in Dudmaston library. Many of the features at The Leasowes were fragile and decayed or disappeared after Shenstone's death, but his ideas continued to be popular, and Dudmaston was among several nearby estates where an existing landscape with a deep valley invited imitation. The Dingle at Badger, north of Bridgnorth, part of a garden created by William Emes for Isaac Hawkins Brown, MP for Much Wenlock, became especially well known.

A wooded link connecting the house to the Dingle is shown in the 1793 watercolour by Moses Griffith, and is also indicated on a map of 1812, although this link had disappeared by 1832. The Dingle later became more densely planted and overshadowed, but originally it was more open, allowing views through and out. A helpful indication of the appearance of the area in the 1830s is found in a series of nine watercolour sketches of the Dudmaston landscape made by Elizabeth Shepherd, a visitor to Dudmaston.

They show an open landscape with individual trees, rather than dense woodland. The National Trust is restoring the historic path network and cascades, and tree thinning is revealing some of the designed views. It is highly likely that Dudmaston's Dingle once had ephemeral features such as seats and shelters, along the line of the rustic structures at The Leasowes and other Picturesque dingles; ongoing research is providing tantalising clues that will help inform future restoration.

Above A 1793 watercolour of the house by Moses Griffith (1749–1819) before the roof and attic storey were transformed in the 1820s

Opposite above One of Elizabeth Shepherd's nine watercolours of the estate in the 1830s

The wider estate

The Dudmaston estate today, in addition to the mansion and its grounds, eight farmhouses and the village of Quatt, consists of 872 hectares (2,155 acres) of agricultural land managed by tenant farmers, and 250 hectares (618 acres) of woodland under the management of the National Trust. Crossed by the Quatt Brook, the gently rising land lies on the east side of the River Severn. The underlying geology is red sandstone, most visible in the 20th-century cuttings made to reduce the gradients on the main road that divides the estate in two.

The name Quatt is derived from Coed, the Celtic word for wood, and its entry in the Domesday Book mentions smallholders who made a living on the cleared fringes. Dudmaston is first named in a deed of c. 1127, although the settlement may be older. In the Middle Ages much of the estate lay on the edge of the Royal Forest of Morfe and was subject to Forest Law. Clearances for agriculture were still subject to fines in the early 17th century; in 1613 Francis Wolryche was fined for making assarts (converting forest to arable use) in the royal forest. The woodland gradually diminished; Morfe Forest became Morfe Heath and was enclosed from the 1780s, but Comer Wood, to the east of the main road, remained an area of traditional forestry practice into the early 19th century, planted with oak, beech and chestnut, later supplemented with conifers.

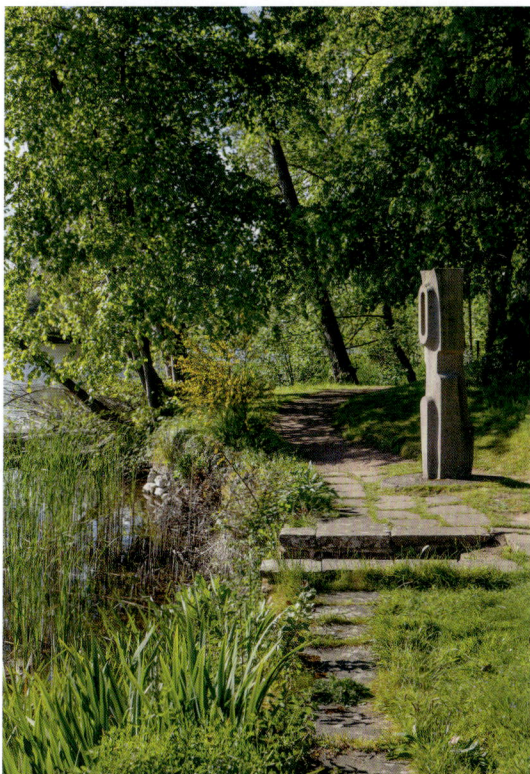

The flora of the valley of the Dingle, close to the mansion, suggests it may in origin be ancient woodland, its steep sides making it impractical for economic forestry. The pleasure grounds created by William and Frances Whitmore from the later 18th century originally extended on both sides of the road, around a series of natural pools. Those west of the road were gradually combined to form Big Pool, close to the mansion (see p.28–9); the pools on the east side formerly had an open outlook to the south.

William Whitmore introduced up-to-date farming methods and began to rebuild the estate farms, such as Lodge Farm in picturesque style. Brick replaced timber or stone, and new farmhouses and outbuildings were set in a landscape of hedged fields, with soil improvement, drainage and the growing of root crops developed to increase productivity. This continued under the following generations of owners.

Opposite A view of the semi-ancient woodlands approaching Belle Vue

Above *The Brewhouse Courtyard* by Evelyn Blacklock (1872–1948), 1914. Frances Evelyn was Geoffrey Wolyrche-Whitmore's sister and married George Blacklock in 1903

Left The wooded path by Big Pool with a sculpture by Anthony Twentyman, *The Watcher*, 1969

Modernising the estate

After the period of agricultural depression between the end of the Napoleonic Wars in 1815 and the 1840s, William Wolryche-Whitmore resumed his father's investment programme.

An industrial school was set up to train the sons of estate workers for a life on the land, and their daughters for dairy and domestic work. Despite the agricultural depression of the later 19th century, improved housing was provided, including a group of attractive cottages at Quatt built in 1871 and designed by John Birch, a London architect specialising in picturesque rural buildings. New lodges, a gate and a boathouse by Big Pool also date from this period.

Radical change came in the early 20th century when Geoffrey Wolryche-Whitmore took over the running of the estate in 1908. Having studied the latest methods of forestry management in Germany, he planted 80 hectares (200 acres) of new woodland in 1910 and built a new sawmill to exploit it.

Until then, all timber had been sawn by hand when the itinerant Earp brothers worked each year for three weeks on the estate.

Geoffrey's interest in trees included ornamental planting; he was among the first in England to grow the dawn redwood (*Metasequoia glyptostroboides*) from seed collected in 1948 after its rediscovery in China. His forestry use of different conifers, such as Douglas fir and Corsican pine, was pioneering (the government's Forestry Commission was only established in

1919) and he became recognised as one of the country's leading experts. It was the planting and harvesting of fast-growing trees that helped Dudmaston to survive during the long economic depression. At the 1951 Festival of Britain, a model of Dudmaston was chosen to demonstrate an estate with integrated farming and forestry. Geoffrey was President of the Royal Forestry Society in 1944–6 and received several of the society's medals, including one of their first Gold Medals, in 1961.

Geoffrey planted fast-growing conifers on the light sandy soil north and west of Comer Wood, where the agricultural land was of poor quality, and mixed them with broadleaf trees on the heavier soil around the pools and in Comer Wood itself. Geoffrey's pioneering work saved Dudmaston. Though it succeeded financially, some of the new and expanded plantings concealed the earlier history of the landscape, leaving the National Trust with a conundrum as to how best to treat these areas.

Right The picturesque
19th-century Gothic
Boathouse, c. 1865, one
of the Victorian
embellishments to
the grounds, built in
Broseley brick after the
enlargement of Big Pool

Opposite The Forestry
medal of the Royal
Agricultural Society of
England, and the Royal
Forestry Society of
England and Wales medal,
Shrewsbury 1949

The management of the house and estate today

Dudmaston was gifted to the National Trust in 1978 by Rachel, Lady Labouchere; after she died in 1996, the mansion, as she had specified, became the family home of her Hamilton-Russell cousins.

Visitors approach the house through the orchard, past the brewhouse and stables with its picturesque Victorian bell-turret. Apples are among the home-grown produce served to visitors. From April to October the main rooms are open to the public, including, most recently, upstairs bedrooms redecorated for the Laboucheres when they moved to Dudmaston in 1968. In the former service wing are the galleries for the collections, ranging from family heirlooms to botanical paintings and Modern Art, which were created by the Laboucheres to provide extra interest for visitors. The National Trust has added a 'Timeline' gallery to illustrate Dudmaston's longevity as a home and how successive members of the family contributed to the development of house and grounds.

Recent work on the estate has been strongly influenced by new research on its different phases. New discoveries continue to be made, with the active help of the team of volunteers, whose assistance is essential in maintaining the garden and grounds. In the Dingle, the original Picturesque concept of views out to the wider landscape is being achieved by thinning the trees, transforming it from woodland to its original form of wood pasture, which can be maintained by grazing. Close to the house, the repair and replanting of the rockery have drawn attention

to both the Picturesque rocky outcrops of sandstone and the Victorian period when the garden was a showpiece for floral displays.

In dealing with the wider estate, the National Trust follows the principles of managed woodland pioneered by Geoffrey Wolryche-Whitmore in the earlier 20th century, and the conifer plantations in the northern parts continue as commercial woodland. In the southern areas around the pools, commercial needs are combined with recovery of historic views. The Trust has its own woodyard and workshop; the use of timber for different purposes, from firewood to carpentry, means that no tree is wasted. This added value enables the estate to be economically sound without pursuing an intensive commercial approach. In order to provide options for a future which may include climate change and tree disease, a broad range of species is cultivated to achieve a mixed, multi-purpose woodland. Paths and bridleways are maintained to enable the public to explore this unique landscape in all its variety throughout the year.

Opposite above Heirloom tricycle

Opposite below Dingle bridge in early autumn

Above The Peacock Room, redecorated by Colefax and Fowler for Lady Labouchere

Dudmaston Family Tree

Owners of Dudmaston are shown in **bold**

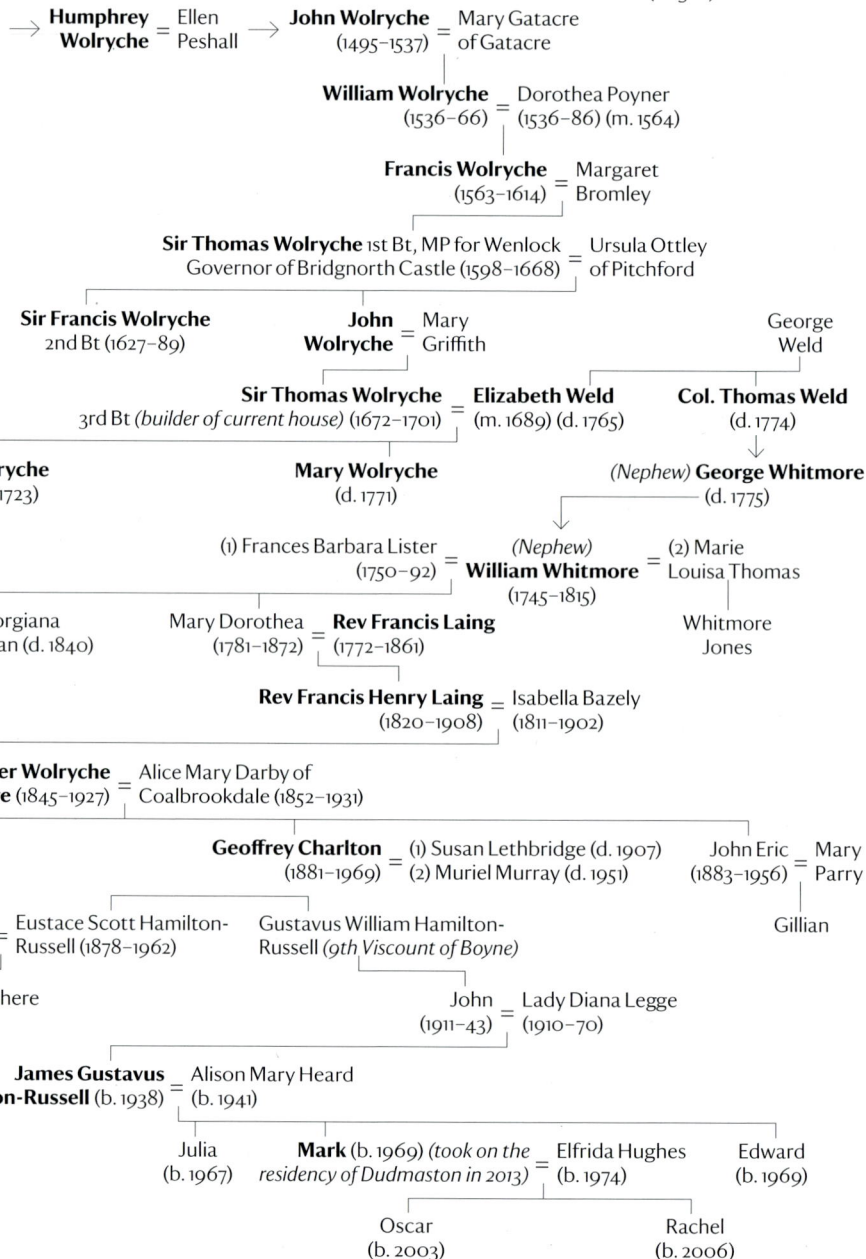

Harlewin de Butailles c.1127 *(changed his name to De Dudmaston)* → **Peter de Dudmaston** → **Hugh de Dudmaston** → **Peter de Dudmaston** → **Hugh de Dudmaston** → **Robert de Dudmaston** → **Richard de Dudmaston** →

→ **Hugh de Dudmaston** → **John de Dudmaston** → **Hugh de Dudmaston** = Margaret (m. 1403) **William Wolryche** — **Andrew Wolryche** = Elizabeth Walton → **Thomas Wolryche** (d. 1502) = Elizabeth Rowley →

→ **Humphrey Wolryche** = Ellen Peshall → **John Wolryche** (1495–1537) = Mary Gatacre of Gatacre

William Wolryche (1536–66) = Dorothea Poyner (1536–86) (m. 1564)

Francis Wolryche (1563–1614) = Margaret Bromley

Sir Thomas Wolryche 1st Bt, MP for Wenlock Governor of Bridgnorth Castle (1598–1668) = Ursula Ottley of Pitchford

Sir Francis Wolryche 2nd Bt (1627–89) — **John Wolryche** = Mary Griffith — George Weld

Sir Thomas Wolryche 3rd Bt *(builder of current house)* (1672–1701) = **Elizabeth Weld** (m. 1689) (d. 1765) — Col. Thomas Weld (d. 1774)

Sir John Wolryche 4th Bt (1691–1723) — **Mary Wolryche** (d. 1771)

(Nephew) **George Whitmore** (d. 1775)

(1) Frances Barbara Lister (1750–92) = *(Nephew)* **William Whitmore** (1745–1815) = (2) Marie Louisa Thomas

Whitmore Jones

William Wolryche Whitmore (1787–1858) = Lucy Georgiana Bridgeman (d. 1840) — Mary Dorothea (1781–1872) = **Rev Francis Laing** (1772–1861)

Rev Francis Henry Laing (1820–1908) = Isabella Bazely (1811–1902)

Francis Alexander Wolryche Whitmore (1845–1927) = Alice Mary Darby of Coalbrookdale (1852–1931)

Frances Evelyn (1872–1948) = George Blacklock — Francis William (1876–8) — **Geoffrey Charlton** (1881–1969) = (1) Susan Lethbridge (d. 1907) (2) Muriel Murray (d. 1951) — John Eric (1883–1956) = Mary Parry

Gillian

Olive Mary (1879–1951) = Eustace Scott Hamilton-Russell (1878–1962) — Gustavus William Hamilton-Russell *(9th Viscount of Boyne)*

Rachel Katherine (1908–96) (m. 1943) = Sir George Peter Labouchere (1905–99) — John (1911–43) = Lady Diana Legge (1910–70)

James Gustavus Hamilton-Russell (b. 1938) = Alison Mary Heard (b. 1941)

Julia (b. 1967) — **Mark** (b. 1969) *(took on the residency of Dudmaston in 2013)* = Elfrida Hughes (b. 1974) — Edward (b. 1969)

Oscar (b. 2003) — Rachel (b. 2006)